BOY SCOUTS OF AMERICA
MERIT BADGE SERIES

PETS

 BOY SCOUTS OF AMERICA®

Requirements

1. Present evidence that you have cared for a pet for four months. Get approval before you start.*

2. Write in 200 words or more about the care, feeding, and housing of your pet. Tell some interesting facts about it. Tell why you have this kind of pet. Give local laws, if any, relating to the pet you keep.

3. Show that you have read a book or pamphlet, approved by your counselor, about your kind of pet.

4. Do any ONE of the following:

    a. Show your pet in a pet show.

    b. Start a friend raising a pet like yours. Help your friend get a good start.

    c. Train a pet in three or more tricks or special abilities.

*Work done for other merit badges cannot be used for this requirement.

35929
ISBN 978-0-8395-3281-1
©2003 Boy Scouts of America
2010 Printing

BANG/Brainerd, MN
5-2010/060092

Contents

The Wonderful World of Pets

Pet ownership is a mixture of fun, excitement, responsibility, commitment, expense, and learning. Besides providing a window into the animal world, owning pets gives us opportunities to participate in activities that strengthen the human-animal bond. Pet ownership teaches us about the responsibility we have to the other living beings on this planet, and pets can be just plain fun. A pet can be our most loyal friend and companion.

When you acquire a pet, you probably are most excited about the thrill of playing with a new animal friend. However, soon you will see that the pet requires nearly the same care as an infant. Overpowering as these new responsibilities might seem, with time, patience, and practice, you and your pet will grow into a team. This will provide the necessary ingredients to make pet ownership a rewarding experience for you and your pet.

If you already have a pet, consider whether you are caring for it in the best possible way. As you read through this merit badge pamphlet, identify what you could be doing differently. Then, with your parents' approval, make changes to improve your pet's quality of life.

Before You Begin

If you are not a pet owner and plan to buy or adopt an animal to earn this merit badge, first give serious thought to pet ownership. You must realize what every *responsible* pet owner already knows: It takes time, effort, and money to care for a pet properly. You must provide food and shelter for your pet. You must ensure quality health care for your pet, which could include vaccinations and preventive and emergency care as needed. You must take the time to properly train your pet so that it does not become a nuisance. You must dedicate yourself to the well-being of a living animal, which means sometimes giving up other activities, such as TV, to tend to your pet's needs.

Consider what type of pet to choose. Understand that different pets require different living arrangements. For example, a large-breed dog will need a large yard and a lot of space for exercise. Municipal laws may restrict the types of pets you keep, and some pets may not be allowed in certain types of homes and apartments. Remember that a Scout is courteous, and keep in mind that good pet owners are always courteous to their neighbors.

When you get a pet, it is a commitment for the *lifetime of the pet,* and you must be prepared to honor that commitment. Your pet might live for quite a long time. Dogs and cats regularly live more than 10 years, and some parrots can live for decades. Do not count on your parents or someone else to finish what you have started just because it is no longer convenient to do so.

Despite what appears to be a long list of things to consider when adding a pet to your life, all of these things can be done. Reading this pamphlet and earning the Pets merit badge will help you learn how to be a good pet owner. Dogs, cats, guinea pigs, hamsters, mice, parakeets, canaries, tropical fish, and goldfish will be discussed in this pamphlet. However, other pets can be used to earn this merit badge. Before you start, discuss with your parents and your merit badge counselor what type of pet you will raise.

Do not keep wild animals such as squirrels, raccoons, or opossums as pets. Wild animals should be left in their natural habitat and enjoyed only when encountered there. Also, wild animals could carry disease and pests such as ticks and fleas.

Puppies and Dogs

There are many things to consider when choosing a dog. First, what kind of dog do you want? A large dog or a small one? Male or female? Is it important that the dog not shed? Where you live will affect your choice. Do you live in an apartment or a house? Will the dog have enough room to exercise? Will the dog stay indoors or outdoors? Is the year-round climate where you live good for the type of dog you want to get?

What other pets do you own, and how will they interact with the new dog? Do you have any special requirements for the dog, such as hunting, hiking, herding, or winter sports?

Whether you get a puppy or an older dog, each will provide challenges and experiences. A puppy must be housebroken, trained, and socialized, but the fun of watching it grow will repay you for the extra effort. An older dog might become homesick, and it might have undesirable habits that will be hard to change. But an older dog probably will be housebroken, and it will have had a least some training and socialization.

Male dogs generally are larger than females of the same breed; otherwise, male and female dogs do not differ in behavior and temperament. Whether you choose a male or female, spay or neuter your dog to help control dog overpopulation.

Dog breeds vary tremendously in shape, size, color, and personality.

Dog Breeds

The American Kennel Club recognizes 150 of the more than 400 breeds found worldwide. Some breeds are quite common and you probably see them often, while others are rare and seldom seen outside of dog shows. Breeds have been developed for thousands of years. Most were developed by different societies to satisfy the specific needs those people had for dogs, such as hunting, guarding, herding, tracking, and racing. Some have been bred for appearance and size. Many purebred dogs have been entered in dog shows and may have a certain degree of worth.

Mixed-breed dogs are mixtures of two or more breeds and may have no outward appearance of any specific breed. However, they are just as loyal and intelligent as purebred animals and just as much fun to raise. A mixed-breed dog usually costs much less than a purebred. However, the care and training needs of purebred and mixed-breed dogs are the same.

Always be prepared to clean up after your dog if it goes to the bathroom while out on your walks.

Longhaired dogs should be combed and brushed after a bath to prevent their hair from matting.

Keep your dog on a regular feeding schedule. This will let you verify that your dog has a healthy appetite. It also will help you house-train your dog.

General Care

When you get your new dog, take it to a veterinarian for a thorough exam. The veterinarian will know which vaccinations and other preventative measures are recommended for a dog in your area. Also, the veterinarian can give advice on proper feeding, grooming, tooth-brushing, and housing needs. Additionally, most veterinarians can give guidance on obedience training, house-training, socialization, and behavior training. If not, they can direct you to someone who can.

All dogs need exercise to stay healthy. If you do not have a large, fenced-in yard, you must take your dog for walks regularly. Large and giant breeds might require an hour of exercise each day. Smaller breeds might do fine with a few daily walks around the neighborhood.

Daily brushing will remove most dirt, debris, and loose hair and is a good practice to begin as soon as you get your dog. Bathe your dog once a month and otherwise only if the dog gets really dirty. Before the bath, place a drop of mineral oil in each eye to prevent soap from causing irritation. Use a commercial dog shampoo unless your dog has a specific need for therapeutic shampoo. Rinse all of the soap out of the dog's hair and then dry the dog thoroughly.

Foot and nail care also is important. Remove dirt or mud clods from between the toes. If this is a problem, you might need to wash the feet often. Some dogs' nails wear down naturally; others must be clipped or filed regularly. Ask your veterinarian how to care for your dog's nails.

Health Care

Depending on the age of your dog, it should be vaccinated regularly for canine distemper, hepatitis, leptospirosis, "kennel cough," canine parvovirus, coronavirus, and rabies. Puppies usually receive a series of vaccinations beginning as early as 6 to 8 weeks of age. This series will require two to four follow-up vaccinations during the first few months to insure good immunity. Rabies vaccination—required by law—is given according to your state's public health guidelines. Boosters to all of these vaccinations will be given throughout your dog's life.

In many areas of the country, dogs can become infected with heartworms, which are spread by mosquitoes. Heartworms can seriously damage your dog's heart, lungs, and quality of life. Your veterinarian can test for heartworms and prescribe the necessary medications. Also, many diseases are spread by ticks and fleas. Good tick and flea control will help eliminate most of these problems.

Feeding Your Dog

Choose a dog food that provides all the nutrients (carbohydrates, fats, minerals, proteins, and vitamins) your dog needs to stay healthy. As a rule, dry dog food is less expensive, easier to store, and plenty healthful for your dog. But if your dog prefers it, you can supplement with semimoist or canned dog food.

Feed an adult dog once or twice a day and puppies several small meals throughout the day. To estimate how much to feed your puppy, weigh the dog. The rule of thumb is 1 cup of dry food for every 20 pounds of body weight per meal. A 5-pound puppy might receive 1/4 cup per meal, three times a day.

Keep plenty of fresh water available at all times. Use a clean bowl or other container, and place it in the shade or where it will stay cool. Check the bowl regularly to make sure it is not empty.

Intestinal worms can be dangerous to puppies. Your veterinarian will examine a stool sample to check for the eggs of intestinal worms common to dogs and then prescribe the proper medication.

Dog Feeding Don'ts

Give your dog only as much food as it will eat. Keeping your dog's bowl filled with dry food might be easier on you, but some dogs will overeat by trying to consume all the food in the bowl. Your dog might become obese if fed this way.

Do not feed a dog pork bones, chicken bones, chop bones, T-bones, or other bones that can splinter. They can cause serious injury. You can give your dog a knuckle bone to chew on—they do not splinter—or a dog toy that is solid enough that your pet cannot chew it up and swallow it.

House-Training Your Dog

A puppy (and older dogs, too!) should be housebroken as soon as possible. Begin the first time you feed your puppy in the morning. Offer food to the puppy for only 10 minutes,

During the first few weeks, take the dog out on a regular schedule: after the puppy wakes up in the morning or after a nap, after meals, when you return after having left the puppy alone, after playing or training sessions, and right before you put the puppy to bed.

then pick up any uneaten food. After the 10-minute feeding period (or less if the puppy eats the meal faster) take the puppy outside. Also take a small portion of the puppy's food with you for a reward. Put the puppy on the ground. When the puppy begins to squat to go the bathroom, say, "Go pottie, go pottie." When the puppy finally goes to the bathroom, praise the puppy lavishly ("Good pottie, good pottie") and give the food reward. These rewards, both vocal and food, will reinforce what you want the puppy to do.

Soon, the puppy will associate the outdoors with using the toilet. Always use the same door and always take your dog to the same general area. This will create patterns in your dog's mind, helping the dog understand what you want it to do.

If there is an accident in the house while you are watching, say "No" firmly but gently so the dog does not become fearful, and immediately take the dog outside. Praise the dog a lot if it uses the toilet outside. Soon, you can depend on your dog's signals to let you know when it has to go outside.

If there is an accident and you are not present, do not punish the dog. Unless the reprimand comes right as it is going to the bathroom, the dog will not connect the accident with the reprimand—and you will only make the dog fearful.

If your puppy soils the carpet, use a biologically active cleaner that eliminates pet odor. You can find these cleaners at your pet supplier. Clean the area immediately. Do not use ammonia products to clean up the mess. Normal cleaners might mask the odor for you, but not for your dog's keen sense of smell. If your dog can still smell the odor, it will likely use the area as a toilet again.

Crate Training

It is a good idea to get a crate in which to confine a puppy. Crates might seem small, but dogs like cozy places of their own. Crates also help house-training because dogs will not go to the bathroom in the same area in which they eat or sleep.

Buy a crate that is just big enough to allow your dog to easily stand up, turn around, lie down, and stretch out. You can buy a crate large enough to fit your dog when it is fully grown, but pad the inside to make the space the right size for your puppy. Otherwise, the space might be large enough that your puppy will use one end as a bathroom.

Until fully house-trained, keep your dog in the crate whenever you are not handling it. This will make house-training easier. Later, you can let the dog out unsupervised, but leave the door open so the dog can return to the crate to rest.

The important thing to remember is that the crate is your dog's safe place. Make it comfortable with soft, washable bedding (not newspaper), and never confine your dog there as punishment.

Socialization

Socializing a puppy with other people and dogs is an important part of helping your pet become well-adjusted to its environment. In nature, litters of wolf puppies and other wild canines interact with other members of their pack. By doing so, they learn how to accept the presence of other animals. Our pets need this same socialization period in their lives.

Try to introduce your new puppy to friends and family members as often as possible. Do not allow anyone to rough-house, tease, or torment your puppy. Instead, have the person hold, pet, give treats, and talk gently and softly to the dog. Remember, good behavior on the part of people will promote good behavior in your puppy.

Sometimes an adopted older dog has not been properly socialized. Learn to observe your older dog for things that seem to bother it. Try gradually introducing the dog to these things a little at time to allow it to become more comfortable. Always praise your dog for anything it does correctly; this will reinforce the dog's good behavior and speed its behavior development.

In extreme weather conditions—hot or cold—bring your dog inside.

Housing Your Dog

Dogs that live outdoors need shelter. If you plan to house your dog outdoors, start when the dog is a puppy. An older dog that is used to being kept indoors will have a hard time adapting to outside living. If you choose an adult dog, find out if it was raised as an outdoor dog before you leave it outside.

An outdoor dog needs a dry, elevated doghouse with clean,

dry bedding and a flap over the entrance to keep out drafts during inclement weather. It should be small enough to allow the dog's body heat to keep the space warm. If you have a garage, consider adding a dog door to the garage and putting a soft cushion in the warmest corner.

If you live in the North, you must give your pet extra care in the winter. Check outdoor water bowls often when the temperature is below freezing. When necessary, break the ice or refill the bowl with warm water.

Dogs living in extremely hot or humid environments need air circulation, plenty of clean, fresh water, and daylong shade. In summertime, be sure to change the water at least twice daily to keep it clean and fresh and free of algae. Dogs can suffer from heat exhaustion and die of heatstroke.

Laws and Ordinances

Know the animal ordinances in your area. You can check with your veterinarian, animal control center, or city police to learn the laws you must follow. Ask your local librarian to help you find them in your city or county code. Some cities have pamphlets outlining your obligations. Pay attention to the law.

Laws regulating animals might include the following:

- **Leash laws.** Many communities require dogs and cats to be leashed in all public areas unless otherwise designated.

- **Pooper-scooper laws.** These laws require owners to pick up and properly dispose of their pet's feces. Violators may have to pay a fine.

- **Licensing laws.** Licenses help your community keep track of pets and let people know whom to call if a pet is lost.

- **Rabies vaccination laws.** These exist in every state.

- **Nuisance laws.** Common nuisance violations include excessive barking or continuous howling and whining.

- **Dangerous or vicious dog laws.** If your dog has caused injury or damage to a pet, person, or property, you may be required to confine or muzzle it, and you may have to insure your dog. In some cases, a dog may have to be destroyed. Also, some household insurance policies will not cover damage or liabilities caused by certain breeds. Have your parents check their homeowner's insurance policy.

- **Breed-specific laws.** These controversial laws single out dog breeds such as Pit Bulls, Rottweilers, Doberman Pinschers, Chow Chows, and others for specific regulations. Some people believe these laws are discriminatory while others believe that certain breeds require additional regulations.

- **Spaying and neutering laws.** These ordinances regulate the breeding of dogs and cats.

- **Wild or exotic animal laws.** Some communities do not allow certain animals, such as skunks, squirrels, raccoons, poisonous snakes, and alligators, to be kept as pets.

Kittens and Cats

Cats are curious. Their curiosity will keep you and your cat entertained for hours. Cats also purr—they hum with affection. Cats come in many sizes and colors. There are tailless cats, longhaired cats, shorthaired cats, large-breed cats, and small-breed cats. There are striped cats, blue cats, yellow cats, black cats, white cats, calico cats, and all colors in between.

With all the different shapes, sizes, and colors, how does one decide what type of cat to get? Well, that is up to you and your pocketbook. Cats can be purchased at pet stores, through cat breeders who might advertise in the newspaper, at your local animal shelter, or maybe from a neighbor with a new litter of kittens. Wherever you get your new cat, like any other pet, it will require full-time care. When selecting a kitten, make sure it is bright-eyed and playful. Avoid kittens with runny noses, runny eyes, and signs of illness, and kittens from dirty quarters.

Cat Breeds

The American Cat Fanciers Association recognizes more than 45 cat breeds. People who show cats professionally generally divide cats into two main groups: longhaired and shorthaired varieties. The shorthaired varieties are further divided into domestic and foreign categories. Most of the cats kept as pets generally are mixtures of various domestic shorthaired varieties.

Cats sleep between 12 and 16 hours a day.

Many differences exist among the purebreds. Breeds such as the Siamese, Oriental, Devon Rex, Cornish Rex, Colorpoint Shorthair, and Balinese are delicate-featured, petite cats. Breeds such as the Maine Coon and the Norwegian Forest are large cats noted for their size and weight. Most cats have a long tail, but the Manx is tailless and the Japanese Bobtail has only a stub of a tail. Most cats have an angular face with a prominent nose and muzzle, but Persian cats have a flat, stubby nose. Most cats have erect, alert-looking ears, while some breeds such as the American Curl and the Scottish Fold have small, irregularly shaped ears. And besides the longhaired and shorthaired varieties, there are curly-haired cats, such as the Selirk Rex, and a completely hairless breed, the Sphynx.

It is a good idea to brush your cat's teeth daily. Ask your veterinarian how.

Health Care

Kittens need vaccinations beginning at 6 to 8 weeks of age and continuing every three to four weeks until they are about 16 weeks old. Common vaccinations include feline distemper, the feline respiratory complex, FIP, FIV, feline leukemia, and rabies. Visit your veterinarian to find out about the vaccinations recommended for your area. Also have your cat checked for internal worms, fleas, and ear mites.

General Care

Cats require only a few supplies. They need a location for their food and water, a secluded place for their litter box, a few toys, a hairbrush or comb, and maybe a scratching post. A cat bed is an option, but cats tend to sleep just about anywhere they feel comfortable.

Good daily brushing can help prevent hairballs, which result when cats swallow large amounts of their own hair.

Brushing your cat's hair will keep it clean and free of mats and debris. Use a soft brush on a kitten and a stiff-bristled brush or a metal comb on an older cat. Brush longhaired cats every day and shorthaired cats about twice a week.

Feeding Your Cat

Good nutrition is important for both active, fast-growing kittens and older cats, but their nutritional requirements differ. Feed kittens a growth formula cat food until they are about 6 months old. Older cats do not need to eat a high-energy growth food like kittens do; these foods might make your older cat gain too much weight. The choice between canned (moist) food and dry food is up to you.

Some people like to leave out food to allow their cat to free-feed all day long. Other cat owners feed their cat at two or three specific times each day, such as once in the morning and once in the evening. Some cats learn to regulate how much they eat; others overeat and become overweight. With a veterinarian's guidance, choose what works best for you and your cat and make adjustments as needed.

If you already have a cat and are introducing a new kitten to your household, put the new arrival in a separate room (like a bathroom), with its food, water, and litter box, for about a week. Remember to spend time with your kitten in this room. This separation time will allow the older cat to adapt gradually to the new kitten, and it will help reduce problems later. After this first week, you can let your kitten out to explore the rest of the house.

Cats enjoy a variety of foods, but do not feed them table food or scraps. Contrary to popular belief, cats do not need milk; however, fresh clean water that is changed daily is a must.

Homes with more than one cat should have multiple litter boxes. A rule of thumb is to have one more litter box than the number of cats in your home.

House-Training Your Kitten

Cats can be trained to use a litter box in a very short time. In fact, most cats prefer to use the litter box as a bathroom. Cats like privacy, so place the litter box in an area where your cat will not be disturbed when using it.

Have a litter box ready in a quiet area, such as a bathroom or laundry room, when you bring your cat home. As soon as you bring the cat into the house, show it the litter box. The cat probably will use the box from the start. If it does not, try to catch the cat when it is looking for a place to go to the bathroom and put it in the litter box. The cat will get the idea.

Fill the litter box 2 to 3 inches deep with litter and clean the box every day. You can use any of a number of different types of cat litter. Some cats prefer gravel litter; others might prefer the types that clump. Similarly, some cats do not like scented litter. You will have to learn from your cat which it prefers.

Some cats prefer to sleep in a place of their own, such as this small basket.

Cats fare better indoors if it is possible for them to stay there. Cats that live outdoors are more likely to get hit by cars, run away, or get into fights with stray cats (which is one way deadly cat diseases are spread).

Cat Habits

Cats, whether living indoors or outdoors, sharpen their claws by scratching on objects. Such an object might be a tree or your family's favorite couch or chair. To prevent unwanted scratching, get a scratching post. You can make one by tacking an old piece of carpet to a post or to a wall next to where the cat likes to sleep. Make the scratching post at least 3 feet tall.

To permanently control scratching, you can have your cat's front claws removed by a veterinarian. Declawed cats still enjoy scratching, but they do not do any damage.

Cats are expert hunters. A cat will stalk prey from an early age if its mother teaches it how. Outdoor cats can become quite proficient in needlessly killing songbirds, however. To help warn prey, put a bell on your cat's collar.

Cats also can be quite skilled at catching mice. Sometimes this is the main reason for owning a cat. An old-time belief that a starved cat would catch more mice is simply not true. A healthy cat is a much better mouser; therefore, never starve a cat hoping it will catch more mice.

Cats in the wild get lots of exercise hunting for food and avoiding predators, but remember that indoor cats need exercise also. Play with your cat daily. Cat toys, such as a small ball or a small stuffed toy on the end of a line, will challenge your cat and give it plenty of exercise. Check your local pet store for a variety of cat toys. Avoid allowing your cat to play with string or yarn. Cats might swallow these items, which might cause severe medical problems.

A license and ID tag on your cat's collar will help you recover your cat if it is lost. Use a "break-away" collar for your cat's safety.

Fish

Raising fish is a fascinating hobby. Just watching fish swim, eat, and court can be entertaining and very relaxing. If you already have an aquarium, you have seen the rare and colorful sight fish provide. If you are a new fish fancier, you are in for a treat.

Tank and Equipment

You will need an aquarium, but it need not be an expensive one. In fact, a secondhand tank works fine if you clean it with water (no detergent or soap) before putting your fish in it. A large rectangular tank is best. Avoid round fishbowls, tall tanks, or narrow-topped aquariums.

Fish need oxygen to survive. Because oxygen dissolves (and carbon dioxide escapes) at the water's surface, the larger the water's surface area the more oxygen will dissolve into the water. Fish bowls with a small water surface area (like goldfish bowls) do not allow carbon dioxide, which will poison your fish, to escape fast enough.

A 10- to 20-gallon rectangular tank is a good size to start. In general, keep 1 inch of cold-water fish per gallon (although goldfish may require 1.5 gallons per inch). You can safely double the number of fish only if you properly aerate the tank. When measuring fish, remember that the length of a fish is measured from the nose to the root of the tail. Do not include the tail fin in your measurements. Allow for fish growth.

Lighting is essential if you plan to keep live plants in your aquarium. A one- or two-bulb reflector will light up your tank. You can buy reflectors or make your own. Fluorescent, incandescent, and other bulb types can be used, and all are satisfactory.

A glass cover or hood will keep fish in and dirt out of your aquarium. Leave a small space open in the hood along the back of the tank to provide access for other aquarium equipment, such as tubes, filters, and heaters. A reflector can be mounted on top of the glass cover.

You will need a dip tube or a siphon and bucket. These items will be used to pick up debris from the bottom of the aquarium and whenever you change the water. Use a dip net to remove fish from the tank. Nylon nets with straight edges are preferred.

That is all the essential equipment you will need to start. But, once the fish bug bites, you probably will want to get more. An air pump, aerator, and filter all are good investments. An aerator is simply an air pump that makes air bubbles in the tank. Air bubbles increase the oxygen exchange in the aquarium. A filter will help keep the tank clean. Filters that fit on the outside of the tank are easiest to clean. If the temperature in your house varies a lot, or if you plan to purchase tropical fish, you will need an aquarium heater with a thermostat.

Make sure your tank sits on a level, sturdy surface.

Lastly, as you become more confident with your aquaculture skills and attempt to raise different kinds of fish, you must learn about monitoring and adjusting the water quality in your aquarium. Testing for and adjusting the pH (acid or base), minerals (the hardness of the water), and chemical levels will be your next step. Aquarium water test kits are available for these needs. Your pet store or merit badge counselor can help you.

A tank thermometer is a must. Fish are sensitive to water temperature, so you will need to monitor the temperature.

Where to Put Your Aquarium

If you do not plan to keep plants in it, you can put the aquarium almost anywhere except in a dark corner, drafty places, or where the temperature fluctuates a lot. Put an aquarium containing plants by a northward-facing window so that the plants and fish get enough light. In nature, fish are used to light filtering through the surface of the water. Try to duplicate these natural conditions as much as possible.

If you plan to landscape your aquarium, you must give your plants something in which to grow, such as sand or gravel. Artificial plants also need a gravel base in which to anchor. A beginner's best bet is the coarse gravel sold in most pet shops. Do not use beach sand. Slope the gravel upward from the back of the tank to the front. Waste will collect at the bottom of the slope, which makes it easier to remove.

Use at least 5 pounds of gravel for a 10-gallon tank.

Underwater Arrangements

Keep metal objects out of your tank. Metal oxidizes in water and can release chemicals that might make your fish ill or kill them. Ceramic ornaments are best and will add to an underwater scene.

Use scenic objects sparingly in your aquarium. A few rocks will spruce up your aquarium, but you will need the right kind. A rock from your garden or another body of water could harm your fish. Buy rocks from a fish dealer. Limestone, seashells, and coral should never be used in a freshwater tank. These rocks will dissolve slowly and change the water quality.

Plants from local ponds or streams can carry parasites and diseases that harm fish. Buy plants from a reliable dealer.

Once the gravel is in place, fill the tank with tap water to a depth of 2 to 4 inches. To add water without disturbing the gravel, place a clean plate over the gravel and pour water carefully and slowly over the plate. Then, remove the plate. Allow the tank to sit for 24 hours to let the water "age." Aging the water allows the chlorine, which is added to tap water to kill microorganisms, to dissipate out of the water.

Next, add plants (live and plastic). Your merit badge counselor can show you how. Some plants have stems that are bunched together. These can remain together as a bunch, but do not plant individual plants in bunches. Also, do not plant them too deep by burying the crown of the plant. Spread the roots after you set the plants, and carefully level the gravel around their bases. Make sure you keep live plants moist while you are working.

An easier and faster approach to "aging" water is to use a dechlorinator (neutralizer), available at most pet shops that carry tropical fish. Follow the manufacturer's instructions carefully, and always use chemicals under the close supervision of an adult.

Once the gravel, plants, and scenic objects are in place, fill the tank with water. Be careful not to dislodge the plants or stir up the gravel—the plate technique works well for this. Now let the tank stand. A newly established tank should stand for about one week before fish are added. This waiting period, besides aging the water, will bring the water to room temperature. If you plan to raise tropical fish, use your aquarium heater to adjust the temperature.

Regardless of how you stock the tank, remember not to overcrowd it. Keep in mind that your fish will grow, too.

Adding the Fish

Acclimate the fish before you add them to the tank. If you do not, the fish may go into shock and die. Turn off the artificial light. Leave the plastic bag containing the fish sealed, and float it in the aquarium 20 to 30 minutes, until the water in the bag reaches the same temperature as the water in the tank. Then open the bag to allow the fish to swim out.

Tropical Fish

There are more than 500 kinds of tropical fish.* These are divided into some 40 different scientific families, which are

divided into genera and further divided into species. As a new aquarist, you probably will hear the common names of the genera, such as barbs, mollies, platys, guppies, bettas, and angelfish.

A lot of new fish fanciers start with a pair of guppies, a pair of mollies, and perhaps a pair of platys, all of which are live-bearers. In addition, you could add some egg-bearers, such as one pair of barbs, zebras, or white clouds. When mixing fish like this, make sure the fish are neighborly and can tolerate the same water temperature and water quality. If you choose schooling fish, you may want to invest in three or more of these so that they are able to school, or swim

Allow 24 hours for the fish to adjust to their new environment. Do not feed the fish during this time. They probably will not eat anything and the food will rot.

*Tropical fish can live in freshwater or saltwater (marine). This merit badge pamphlet covers only those tropical fish that live in freshwater. Raising marine tropical fish is an exciting world of color, equipment, and expertise that you may want to explore as your interest in raising fish expands.

in a group—they will be much happier. Choose fish that are around the same size, even if they are different species.

Buy fish from a good dealer— your merit badge counselor can tell you where to find one. Avoid bargain buys. Make sure the fish you buy look healthy. Select only fish that appear vibrant and active.

You can specialize and keep one type of fish, or you can start with a community tank—a tank with small numbers of different fish.

Food and Feeding

Fish food commonly comes in flakes, but it also comes frozen, live, and in pellets. Feeding different forms and types of food provides variety that is more like what fish experience in the wild.

Try to feed fish twice daily at the same times each day, putting the food into the same area of the aquarium each time. The fish will get used to the schedule. If you can only feed once daily, do it in the morning.

Feed only enough that almost all the food is gone in five minutes. This will help your fish stay healthy, because overfeeding can cause disease. Excess food settling on the bottom of your tank will also pollute the water, so feed small amounts to help your tank stay clean.

Do not let anyone who does not know how to care for fish feed yours when you are away. It is OK not to feed your fish if you are gone for a weekend. If you will be away longer than that, measure out the food for each day so that the fish will not be overfed. Remember, a feast is worse than a famine as far as fish are concerned.

Some fish lay eggs; they are called egg-bearers. Live-bearers do not lay eggs. Instead, the female hatches eggs within her body, and the babies, called *fry*, appear only when they are fully formed.

If feeding frozen food to your fish, make sure it has been pasteurized. Plain freezing does not kill all bacteria and parasites, which can infect your aquarium.

Before you buy a type of fish, find out what kind of food it needs. Flesh-eating and plant-eating fish need different types of protein. Also, some fish will only eat live food.

The *Synodontis courteti,* a spotted catfish, comes from West Africa.

General Care

Make sure to keep the tank clean. A filter will help, but it must be cleaned every week. Use a siphon to remove the food and droppings that accumulate in the bottom of the tank. Water that is a little green will not harm your fish, but when it gets soupy and opaque, you had better change it. Additionally, you also must replace water that evaporates over time. Age the new water overnight before adding it to the tank, or use a chemical dechlorinator (under the close supervision of an adult).

A helpful, little, live vacuum cleaner for any tank is a small catfish. It will eat bits of food that other fish miss. Catfish also help keep a tank clean, but do not depend on them to do the entire job. They can only do so much, and they can suffer from overeating also.

This species of the Apple snail, called the *Pomacea bridgesi,* is a good choice for aquariums.

Snails also will help with housecleaning. They eat leftover food and the algae that grows on the side of the tank and on your plants. Popular snails are the Japanese snail, the mystery snail, and the red ramshorn. But do not neglect these small scavengers: If a snail dies it might cloud and poison the water. Be aware that some species of snails readily reproduce and can quickly overpopulate an aquarium.

You might want to add new fish to an established tank, especially after some of your fish die. First, isolate and treat any diseased fish in a small separate tank. If you had sick fish in your main tank, consider cleaning the entire tank and changing the water to prevent disease from spreading to the new fish. Second, check your new fish for signs of disease. Quarantine the new fish in a separate tank for at least one week. This will ensure that your tank does not become contaminated. Then, just before you add the new fish to the tank, feed your "regulars." Float the plastic bag containing the new fish in the aquarium until the two water temperatures are the same. Then let the fish swim out.

Health Hints

"Ich," short for Ichthyophthirius, is the most common protozoal disease of tropical fish. It is also known as the "salt and pepper" disease. A newly infected fish has white specks on its fins and body. A fish with an advanced case looks as if it has been sprinkled with salt and pepper. Infected fish shake, become thin, and eventually drop to the bottom. A sudden drop in water temperature or a chill seems to cause the disease. To get rid of it, gradually raise the water temperature to about 85 degrees. You can buy remedies from a fish dealer, but you must follow the directions exactly.

If the water in the tank turns green or gets cloudy, you might need to feed less or keep fewer fish. Overcrowding and overfeeding are the most common causes of dirty water.

Saltwater Cure

The saltwater cure can be used for Ich and other diseases, but before you try this method, be sure your fish will tolerate the salt. Put your diseased fish in a container of warm salt water. Make the salt water by mixing 1 tablespoon of aquarium salt (not iodized table salt) in 5 gallons of aged or aquarium water. Keep the diseased fish in the salt water until they are cured. The exact time will vary with the fish. If the water starts to smell stale, put the fish into new salt water. Clean the tank before returning the cured fish. Sterilize your dip net after using it with a sick fish.

Goldfish

Goldfish and their relative, the koi, have been kept as pets in Asia for centuries. You usually can find five or six varieties of gold-fish for sale at pet shops, but there are about 20 kinds—some costing as much as several thousand dollars apiece. The fantail, comet, and nymph are common breeds. Fancier breeds include round-bodied veiltails; fringetails, which have long fins and tails; bulging-eyed telescopes and celestials; lionheads; and the Chinese moors.

The fancier breeds of goldfish, such as this Oranda, usually are not as hardy as the common types.

When you buy goldfish, check each one carefully. Each fish should have good, bright color. If it is speckled with white dots, coated with scum, swims on its side, or seems the least bit sluggish, look for a better fish in *another* tank. Size does not indicate the health of a fish.

General Care

Feed goldfish prepared food made specifically for goldfish. Flakes are adequate and you can feed a variety of types— one type one day and one type another day. Feed once daily, preferably in the morning. Feed only enough so that almost all the food is gone in five minutes. Excess food will settle on the bottom of your tank and pollute the water.

Goldfish fare best in 60-degree water, but they will do well at temperatures between 55 and 70 degrees. However, they cannot take a sudden change in water temperature. When adding aged water, let it stand until it is the same temperature as the water in the aquarium.

If you use an aerator and filter, your tank will stay reasonably clean. But goldfish generate a lot of waste, so remember to clean the filter every week. If you do not use a filter, you must remove food and droppings from the bottom of the aquarium with a dip tube. When the water begins to look dirty, exchange some of the water with aged water.

If you do not use an aerator, you must make sure the water contains adequate oxygen. Live plants will supply some oxygen, but probably not enough. If your fish are always near the water's surface and moving their gills faster than usual, they probably need more oxygen. This is a sign you need to change at least part of the water. In warmer months you may need to change the water more regularly, or consider purchasing an aerator.

Health Hints

Fin congestion and white fungus are two common goldfish diseases. Overfeeding causes fin congestion. Sudden chill, or low or high temperatures for an extended time also cause this disease. An affected fish will have red or bloodshot fins. Reduce the stress on the fish by limiting food and stabilizing the tank temperature. You also can use the saltwater cure mentioned earlier. White fungus attacks weakened or bruised goldfish. You can spot the white spores of this disease on the fins or on a bruise. Treatment is limited to isolation in a separate tank and the saltwater cure.

Birds

Are you "for the birds" as far as having a pet? You have a wide choice—canaries, tame crows, cockatiels, mynah birds, lovebirds, parrots, pigeons, peacocks, parakeets, toucans, and others. Any one of them will make a good pet. Of course, along with the variety of choices comes a variety of life spans, costs, housing requirements, and safety concerns, but also a wide range of personalities that make endless hours of fun and companionship.

Whichever bird you choose, find out as much as you can about it before you buy. Books and pamphlets on all types of birds are available at pet stores, at libraries, and on the Internet. In this chapter, you will find tips and hints on how to raise the two most popular choices among bird lovers, the parakeet and canary.

Parakeets

For a bird that is easy to care for and learns tricks quickly, the inexpensive pocket-sized parrot, the parakeet, is ideal. Also called the keet, budgie, and budgerigar, the parakeet is a colorful bird native to Australia. This bird also talks, like its cousin the parrot. It is curious, cocking its little head to study everything it encounters. It also is a mimic, acrobat, and comedian.

Parakeets live an average of six years, with the record being 18 years.

Budgies can be divided into three basic color groups: green, blue, and yellow. Each of these is divided into shades. The greens, for example, are called light, dark, and olive.

Don't let the colors confuse you. Colors have nothing to do with a parakeet's personality or abilities. Younger birds might appear duller in color, but soon they will molt (lose their feathers) and develop brilliantly colored adult plumage.

To your budgie, a cage without a perch would be like a house without a chair. Place round hardwood perches where the budgie can reach food and water easily. Avoid wooden perches wrapped in sandpaper because these might irritate the bird's feet. Later, you can add accessories, such as a ladder. A little bell hung from the side of the cage and a small mirror make nice toys.

Budgies also have different color markings: cinnamon, black, and gray. There are albinos (all white), too. A lutino is a yellow budgie with red eyes. Budgies with white or yellow patches are called pieds or harlequins. Males can be differentiated from females by the presence of a lavender to dark blue "cere" above the beak; the cere on a female is usually brown or tan.

When purchasing a parakeet, look for a healthy, lively bird. It should be at least 5 weeks old. Buy only from a dealer with a good reputation. Make sure birds in cages adjacent to the bird in which you are interested appear healthy and lively also. Both male and female budgies make good pets. It is better to purchase only one budgie. A single bird will be more attentive to you and will learn faster than if it had a partner.

Cages

Some people let their birds have the run of the house, but this habit is risky, especially if you have ceiling fans and open windows. Get a roomy cage, one that is at least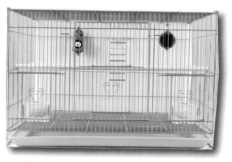
1 foot by 2 feet and 18 inches high. An oblong cage is best. Avoid rounded cages because the space between the bars narrows at the top, which could trap your bird's head and neck. A cage with a removable bottom tray and removable food cups is recommended. Make sure these cups are within easy reach because you will add food and change the water daily. Two doors having secure, not sliding, latches are preferred. A plastic guard around the lower part of the cage will help keep seeds and dirt from being pushed out.

Hang the cage from a wall or a ceiling bracket, or simply set it on a secure table. Wherever you put the cage, try to keep the highest level that the bird can reach below the height of your head. This will keep the bird from thinking it is dominant. Keep the cage out of drafts and full sunlight. Avoid placing the cage in the kitchen, and of course, keep the cage out of the reach of dogs and cats.

When you are ready to introduce the budgie to its new home, take out all but the bottom perches in the cage. This will force the bird to perch close to its food and water. Lastly, always cover the cage at night with a sheet, or something similar, that has a ventilation hole at the top. Birds fare best on a 12-hour daylight/12-hour nighttime cycle.

Cover the cage at night to keep the bird quiet and to mimic the natural day/night cycle birds experience in nature. Make sure the cover leaves an air space at the top of the cage.

Feeding

Your budgie probably will not eat when you first bring it home, but feed it anyway. Also scatter some seed on the floor around the food cup. You might notice that your budgie acts a little drowsy the first day. Don't worry, this is a normal reaction.

Feed your budgie a parakeet seed mix. Give the budgie fresh, clean seed and fresh water every morning. Your bird will eat the seeds and leave the husks (the seed coverings); keep the food cup free of hulls and full of seeds. Occasionally stir the seed in the food cup to keep the seeds exposed to air. Feed young budgies crushed seeds for the first few weeks.

Supplement your bird's diet with small treats, such as finely chopped dark green or dark yellow vegetables and fruits. Bread, macaroni, cooked egg, and millet seeds also can be used. During breeding or molting, your bird might need special foods. Ask your veterinarian for recommendations.

General Care

Your new budgie might need some time to get used to your home. Cover the cage with a cloth for several hours during the first day to help reduce the stress and confusion of the new surroundings. Perhaps the most important thing you can do is leave your pet alone until it gets settled.

Keep a cuttle-bone in the cage. This chalky white bone provides neces-sary calcium for your bird. It also will help keep the budgie's beak trim.

You will need to trim your bird's nails from time to time. A veterinarian can show you how to do this using an emery board.

Avoid putting the cage next to an air conditioner duct or in front of a window when the weather is cold because cold drafts might make your budgie sick. Putting the cage across the room from a window is fine; the window will provide entertainment for the bird.

Budgies preen to stay clean. Preening is when a bird combs and grooms itself with its beak and feet. Your budgie also might take a bath. It might like to splash around in a shallow dish of water, fluff its feathers when misted lightly with water, or roll around in wet lettuce leaves. Try each method to see which one your bird prefers, but do it only in the morning. A budgie's feathers should never be wet when it settles down for the night.

Empty the bottom tray every day. Wash the tray with hot water and soap at least once a week. Wash out the water and food cups daily. Make sure to thoroughly rinse and dry them. Do not wash the perches; occasionally scrape them clean with a knife.

If you want to let your bird fly loose in your home, first bird-proof the room you in which you will release it. Close all drapes and blinds to prevent it from flying into a window. Turn off all fans, including ceiling fans. Remove all dogs and cats from the room.

Some bird owners clip their bird's wings to prevent flying. However, a bird with clipped wings might be able to fly for short distances. If you wish to have your bird's wings clipped, a veterinarian can help you. But be vigilant about the bird's flying abilities as the wing feathers begin to grow out.

Health Hints

Budgies are hardy little birds. However, they are susceptible to colds brought on by excessive chill, rough handling, and con-taminated, spoiled, or moldy food or water. Exposure to other sick birds is another source of infection. A common sign of ill-ness is a bird with its feathers fluffed up continuously. If your bird appears sick, keep the bird warm (85 to 90 degrees) and take it to a veterinarian immediately. Mites found on the beak, feet, skin, and feathers are another problem for bird owners. A veterinarian can recommend treatments for your bird, while treatment for the bird's environment can be done at home. You can cleanse the empty cage and equipment by immersing them in boiling water.

Bird Handling Tips

You might want to pick up and handle your bird on occasion. Do it carefully. Slowly insert your hand into the cage so as not to frighten your pet. Pick up the bird from the rear. Put your hand over its back and your fingers and thumb around its neck. Hold the bird loosely— do not squeeze it.

To finger train your bird, put your extended index finger in front of its feet. Slowly push against the bird. It might move away or nip. However, be persistent. It might take some time for the bird to finally step up on your finger. Training sessions should be limited to 15 minutes or less, two or three times a day.

Canaries

Canaries were discovered on the Canary Islands, hence the name. Pet-shop canaries are related to the wild canaries found on those islands centuries ago. Through careful breeding, they have developed better singing abilities and more color patterns.

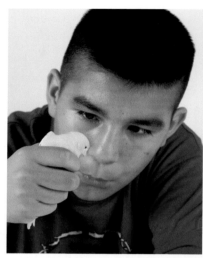

A singing canary is a cheerful pet that can live for 15 years or more.

There are some 50 varieties of canaries. For ease of discussion, canaries are divided into two general groups: canaries bred for appearance (fancy-colored canaries) and canaries bred for singing. The "fancies" come in pink and orange-red shades. Additionally, some have feathered crests that look like wigs, while others have curly feathers. Some are even fed food coloring to turn their feathers different colors.

Canaries are famous for their singing. Singing varieties include rollers (soft, rolling melodies), choppers (loud singers), and warblers. If you want a bird that sings, buy a male that is younger than 2 years old. Females seldom do more than chirp or sing a few simple trills.

Pick a healthy, lively bird, one with good, bright, feathers. Make sure birds in cages adjacent to the one in which you are

If you bring the canary home in a traveling box, fasten the box to the cage and let the bird enter on its own. Cover the cage with a cloth or newspaper. Drafts and the excitement of a new environment can be stressful for your bird.

interested appear healthy and lively also. Listen to the songs of the different birds at the shop, then pick the bird whose song you like best. Purchase your canary only from a dealer with a good reputation.

Cages

Buy a rectangular cage, not a round one, because the shape is more comforting to canaries and provides more room in which to fly. The minimum size should be 12-by-12-by-10 inches. Initially, put perches only near the food and water cups. You may add additional perches once your canary is used to the location of its food and water. Keep in mind, however, that too many perches will interfere with flying space. Likewise, one or two playthings are enough. Use unpainted perches of different thicknesses, and put them where they will not get wet.

Hang the cage from a wall or a ceiling bracket, or simply set it on a table. Wherever you put the cage, try to keep the highest level that the bird can reach below the height of your head. This will keep the bird from thinking it is dominant.

Never keep a bird near a kitchen where nonstick cooking pans will be used. If overheated, the nonstick surface releases toxic fumes that will kill your bird.

Avoid using synthetic nesting fibers. These items might entangle the feet, toes, or other small body parts of your canary. Safe nesting material can be purchased at a pet store.

To encourage your pet to sing, put the cage in good day-time light but never where it will be in the sun all day. Also, avoid drafts from ceiling fans and household air vents, which will chill and stress your bird. Avoid placing the cage in the kitchen, and of course, keep the cage out of the reach of dogs and cats. Lastly, always cover the cage at night with a sheet, or something similar, that has a ventilation hole at the top. Birds fare best on a 12-hour daylight/12-hour nighttime cycle.

Feeding

Feed 1 tablespoon of a fresh canary seed mixture per bird daily. Buy good, formulated canary seed. Pelleted diets are available for canaries, too. Have a cuttlebone and fresh, clean water in the cage at all times. Change the water and clean the water cup twice daily. Once a month, sprinkle ¼ teaspoon of gravel (purchased at a pet store) on the bottom of the cage. Canaries eat the gravel, which helps them digest food.

An occasional eggshell is good for canaries. Crush the shell from a boiled egg and put it in the cage. Some mashed yolk of a hard-boiled egg is also good. A small slice of ripe apple or sweet orange can be given every day.

General Care

Because canaries are easily startled, make sure the canary knows when you approach the cage. Whistle or talk to your canary to let it know the direction from which you are coming.

Your canary will bathe if you give it a shallow dish of water. Set it on the bottom of the cage. Do this in the morning, so the feathers will be dry by evening, and no more than twice a week.

Empty the bottom tray every day. Wash the tray with hot water and soap at least once a week. Wash out the water and food cups daily. Make sure to thoroughly rinse and dry them. Do not wash the perches; occasionally scrape them clean with a knife.

Health Hints

Canaries are tropical birds that like warm environments. They are susceptible to chills, which can lead to illness. Other stresses include rough handling and contaminated, spoiled, or moldy food or water.

Exposure to other sick birds is another source of infection. A common sign of illness is a bird with its feathers fluffed up continuously. If your bird appears sick, keep the bird warm (85 to 90 degrees) and take it to a veterinarian immediately.

Mites found on the beak, feet, skin, and feathers are another problem for bird owners. A veterinarian can recommend treatments for your bird, while treatment for the bird's environment can be done at home. You can cleanse the empty cage and equipment by immersing them in boiling water.

Some birds have identification bands on their lower legs. If your bird has such a band, inspect it daily to make sure it is not causing irritation. If leg swelling develops, immediately take your bird to a veterinarian to have the band removed.

Pocket Pets

Looking for a small pet—one you can hold in your hands, teach tricks, and leave in a cage when you are away? Then consider a hamster, guinea pig, or mouse. These pets are affectionately called "pocket pets" because they actually can be carried in your pocket. These types of animals make great apart-ment companions, if it is OK with your landlord.

Guinea Pigs

A guinea pig is not a pig, it is a rodent. Guinea pigs are 6 to 9 inches long and weigh about 2 pounds at adulthood. They have four toes on the front feet, but only three toes on each hind foot. They also lack a tail. They live an aver-age of five years.

A relative of the porcupine, the guinea pig is native to South America and is commonly known as a cavy (rhymes with navy).

While three breeds of guinea pigs—English, Abyssinian, Peruvian—are common, most people raise the English, or smooth-haired, guinea pigs. English come in a variety of colors and require less daily care than the other breeds. The Peruvian, with long straight hair, and the Abyssinian, with rough wiry hair, require daily brushing.

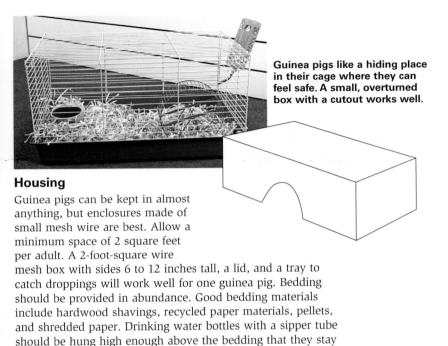

Guinea pigs like a hiding place in their cage where they can feel safe. A small, overturned box with a cutout works well.

Housing

Guinea pigs can be kept in almost anything, but enclosures made of small mesh wire are best. Allow a minimum space of 2 square feet per adult. A 2-foot-square wire mesh box with sides 6 to 12 inches tall, a lid, and a tray to catch droppings will work well for one guinea pig. Bedding should be provided in abundance. Good bedding materials include hardwood shavings, recycled paper materials, pellets, and shredded paper. Drinking water bottles with a sipper tube should be hung high enough above the bedding that they stay clean and free of debris. Use a small ceramic food bowl.

A room temperature of 55 to 70 degrees is best for a guinea pigs. Temperatures above 85 degrees may cause heatstroke, and temperatures below 50 degrees are too cold. Also, it is important to protect your guinea pig from drafts and moisture. You can house your guinea pig outdoors if the temperature is right. Keep the guinea pig separated from other pets, and make sure mice and rats cannot invade its cage and food.

When you purchase a guinea pig, make sure it is at least 6 weeks old and comes from a reliable dealer with a clean pet shop.

Guinea pigs require a dietary supplement of vitamin C. You can add vitamin C directly to the drinking water (mix 50 milligrams of vitamin C with 8 ounces of water). Pieces of an orange or a small handful of cabbage, kale, or parsley given daily also provide vitamin C.

Sipper tube

Feeding

Use commercial guinea pig food (containing 20 percent protein and 16 percent fiber), and store it in a sealed container to keep it fresh. Guinea pigs also like to eat hay. Carrots, celery tops, alfalfa cubes, green vegetables, and apples can be given as treats, but they should be limited to no more than 1 or 2 tablespoons per 24-hour period. Too many treats can give a guinea pig diarrhea. If diarrhea develops, stop the treats until the droppings appear normal. Then gradually reintroduce the treats in smaller amounts than before.

General Care

Make sure to keep your guinea pig's cage clean and dry. Change the bedding every two days. Thoroughly clean the pen with soap and water at least twice a week. Change the water and clean the water bottle and sipper tube daily. A clean, large pipe cleaner works well to clean the sipper tube. The food bowl also must be cleaned daily.

Brush shorthaired guinea pigs weekly and longhaired breeds daily. The teeth and toenails might need occasional trimming or filing to prevent overgrowth. A veterinarian can assist you with these tasks.

Handle your guinea pig often, but do so gently. Guinea pigs do not often bite, but they will if handled roughly. When you hold your guinea pig, put one hand under it and the other hand around its shoulders for support.

Health Hints

Guinea pigs most commonly develop medical problems involving the respiratory system, skin, and digestive system. If your pet shows signs of sickness, such as breathing difficulties, bedraggled fur, loss of appetite, a discharge from the nose or eyes, or a tendency to bury its head in a corner and remain inactive for long periods, isolate the guinea pig and contact your veterinarian. Help prevent disease by keeping the pen clean, feeding the proper diet, providing fresh clean water, and keeping the quarters dry and draft-free.

Hamsters

Hamsters are active, athletic, entertaining little balls of fur. These rodents are native to Asia and Europe, where they are pests that burrow under farmland. They love to hoard things and store great piles in their nests. They usually are clean and do not require much grooming. Hamsters are nocturnal and probably sleep more during the day than other pocket pets. However, they can be escape artists and must be kept in secure cages. They live about two years and grow to about 6 inches long.

Hamsters come in many colors and with a variety of hair lengths. The golden hamster comes in shorthaired and long-haired varieties. There are also Chinese, European, and Hungarian varieties.

Housing

Adult hamsters need at least a 2-foot-square enclosure that is at least 10 inches high. The best home for your hamster would be made of wire mesh with a solid floor of plastic or aluminum. A cage like this is easiest to clean and will provide good ventilation. Avoid cages made from too much wood, plastic, or soft metal, as hamsters are strong chewers and good escape artists. A 10-gallon glass aquarium is OK if it has a securely fastened lid. If you use an aquarium, make sure the lid is made of wire mesh to allow proper ventilation.

Exercise balls provide good opportunities to interact with your hamster, guinea pig, or pet mouse. However, these must be used only under constant, close supervision so that your pet does not get injured.

Cover the floor of the cage with bedding, such as hardwood shavings, recycled newspaper, or pellets, to a depth of 1 to 2 inches. Hamsters will enjoy a separate sleeping box (about 4 inches square) attached to the side of the cage. Put in a small ladder to let the hamster climb into its box. Also, your hamster might enjoy playing on an exercise wheel.

Water bottles with a sipper tube should be hung high enough above the bedding that they stay clean and free of debris. Clean the bottle and sipper tube daily. A clean, large pipe cleaner works well to clean out the sipper tube.

The ideal temperature for a hamster is between 65 and 70 degrees. Prolonged temperatures below 55 degrees will cause your hamster to hibernate.

Feeding

Feed a commercial hamster diet that contains at least 16 percent protein. Do not feed seed-type pet mixes because the hamster will pick out only the foods it wants and hoard (bury) the rest. Hamsters tend to stuff their cheeks with food and then store it away. Hoarded food will only spoil and rot, and you must remove it from the cage regularly. You can give your hamster treats of salad sprouts, walnuts, raisins, various salad greens, and small bits of apple, but these should be limited to no more than $1/2$ teaspoon per 24 hours. Too many treats might upset the digestive system. If this occurs, discontinue these foods for a few days.

A hamster's front teeth grow continuously and normally are worn down by chewing on hard items. You can give your hamster small pieces of dog biscuit or natural wood chew sticks to help wear down the teeth. Because hamsters are nocturnal, plan to serve meals in the late afternoon or early evening. Keep fresh, clean water available in a regularly cleaned sipper bottle.

General Care

Hamsters will wash themselves, but you will have to wash and clean the cage once a week. Change the bedding twice a week and remove all droppings and hoarded food. If your hamster is nesting with babies, mix some of the used bedding with the new bedding you add. However, it is best to leave your hamster alone when she has a litter. Limit your cleaning to once every two weeks, if possible, until the babies are weaned.

Hamsters like to be handled, and the more you handle them the tamer they get. However, they may bite if startled, handled roughly, or abruptly awakened from a sound sleep. Do not surprise your hamster. Let it know you are coming, and pick it up gently by scooping up the animal. Put your other hand under it to cradle its body.

Health Hints

Like most pocket pets, hamsters most commonly develop medical problems involving the respiratory system, skin, and digestive system. If your pet shows signs of sickness,

Generally, hamsters do better as solitary pets. Mixing males and females, besides creating lots of baby hamsters, might lead to hamster fights.

Diarrhea, sometimes called "wet tail," is a serious condition that requires veterinary attention.

such as breathing difficulties, bedraggled fur, loss of appetite, a discharge from the nose or eyes, and long periods of inactivity, isolate the hamster and contact your veterinarian. Help prevent disease by keeping the cage clean, feeding the proper diet, providing fresh water, and keeping the quarters dry and draft-free.

Mice

Mice are lively little pets. There are many different breeds available in a range of colors including white, black, tan, and brown. Mice are also escape artists, and they are active both day and night. If you decide to get more than one mouse, start with two females and one male. Males might fight initially when caged together. Mice live about two years.

Housing

Mice are easier to house than other pocket pets. Usually, 1 square foot per adult mouse is sufficient. A female with a litter requires about two to three times as much space.

You can house mice in wire mesh or plastic enclosures, or a converted aquarium with a secure wire mesh lid. Whichever you use, make it large enough to accommodate feeding and nesting areas, an exercise wheel, and other toys such as a paper towel tube. Provide adequate bedding, such as hardwood shavings, shredded recycled paper, shredded paper, or pellets. Cedar and pine shavings are not recommended for mice. Shredded, unscented paper towels, tissue paper, and old socks and mittens also make excellent nesting materials. Mice do well at room temperatures of 65 to 85 degrees.

Mice are great climbers and will enjoy multiple levels and tubes in their mouse house.

A small ceramic food container and a water bottle designed for mice that hangs from the side of the cage are a must and need to be cleaned daily.

Feeding

Feed a commercial rodent mix that contains at least 14 percent protein. Avoid seed-based diets and sweets, veggies, salt blocks, and liquid vitamins. Occasionally, treats such as crumbled dog biscuits, bread crusts, and small bits of apple, carrot, or lettuce may be given. Do not give your mice meat; it may make them cannibalistic and smelly. Make sure the food bowl always contains food. Mice demand a lot of energy and will starve quickly if food is not available. Never let them go more than 20 hours without food.

Cheese? Never, Please!

Believe it or not, cheese is not good for mice. Feed only commercial rodent food mix.

General Care

Mice love to chew, so give them pieces of hardwood to chew on.

Thoroughly clean the cage once a week, and change the bedding at least weekly. Mice mark their territory with scent, which the bedding absorbs. If you replace all of the bedding at once and too often, the mice might become uncomfortable. Instead, when you replace the bedding, leave some of the old bedding in the cage.

You can handle your mice, but do it gently because they are very small and fragile. Pick up a mouse by simultaneously grasping the loose skin on the neck and the base of the tail. Then place the mouse in your hand.

Mice move quickly and can run from your hand up your arm with surprising speed. Be careful never to drop a mouse on the floor. Your mouse might pass some droppings or urinate in your hand while you hold it. Therefore, always wash your hands after handling mice.

Health Hints

Mice are hardy pets. Keeping the cage clean will minimize odors and help keep mice healthy. If one of your mice appears sick (breathing difficulties, bedraggled fur, loss of appetite, a discharge from the nose or eyes, long periods of inactivity), immediately isolate it in a separate cage and consult your veterinarian. Meanwhile, disinfect the mouse's cage and change the bedding.

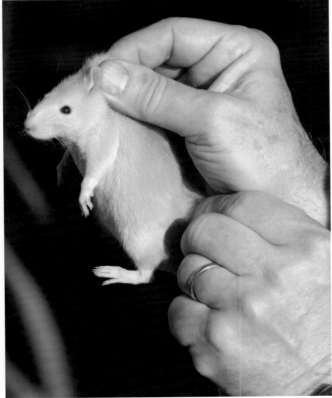

As your mouse gets used to you, it might just crawl into your hand so you can pick it up.

Breeding, Training, and Showing

Pets are a pleasure to have and enjoy. But with many pets, you can have the added pleasure of breeding and training them. Cats and dogs can be exhibited in official cat and dog shows, while any animal can be exhibited at an ordinary pet show.

Some pets cannot be bred. The common pet turtle, for example, does not normally mate and breed in captivity. Some pets cannot be trained. Fish are a good example. However, all pets can be shown at some type of pet show, and any pet is likely to arouse the interest of another person.

> With your experience, you can teach a friend how to raise a pet like the one you have.

Should You Breed a Cat or Dog?

Every year millions of puppies and kittens are born in the United States. Unfortunately, many of them will never find a home. Litters of unwanted animals are sometimes abandoned or dumped along road-sides when their owners move or are tired of caring for them. It is estimated that more than 20 million cats and dogs enter the nation's animal shelters each year. Fewer than 20 percent of these animals are ever adopted or claimed by their owners. The sad reality is that many are put to death because no one wants them. Additional millions of abandoned animals never make it to shelters, where they at least have a chance of adoption. Instead, they spend their lives roaming city streets and country roads, dying of starvation, disease, and exposure.

You can help solve the problem of pet overpopulation and prevent the death of unwanted animals. First, be a responsible pet owner. Do not buy or adopt an animal unless you are committed to properly caring for the pet throughout its lifetime. You must be willing to exercise, feed, groom, train, socialize (dogs), attend to the medical needs of, and otherwise spend time with your pet according to the animal's needs and not your own convenience.

People who leave an animal alone in an apartment or house for long periods and neglect to feed or exercise it wind up with a frustrated, lonely, and badly behaved pet instead of the affectionate companion they wanted. It is these animals that often are abandoned or taken to the shelter to be put to sleep. Be sure you understand that when you bring a pet into your home, it becomes your responsibility. In return, your pet will give you years of faithful companionship and love.

Second, have your pet spayed or neutered so it cannot reproduce. Cats and dogs that are allowed to breed freely are the root of the pet overpopulation problem. According to Spay/USA, 70,000 puppies and kittens are born each day. Millions of unwanted dogs, cats, kittens, and puppies are destroyed by animal control agencies each year.

One female dog or cat can give birth to a dozen or more puppies or kittens every year. If you let your pet breed, you might find homes for that first litter, but what happens when each of those puppies or kittens has a litter of its own? Counting all the descendants, one cat or dog can add thousands of new animals to the pet surplus during its lifetime.

There are many advantages to having your cat or dog spayed or neutered. Spaying a female will reduce her risk of getting cancer and will keep barking male dogs or yowling tomcats from invading your yard when she is in heat. Neutered males are less likely to get into fights, and tend to be more affectionate. A tomcat neutered when young is less likely to develop the habit of spraying urine and marking territory in your home.

Neutering will not make your pets fat and lazy, as people commonly believe. Overeating and lack of exercise do that. Neutering helps your pet live a longer and healthier life and gives you a more affectionate and manageable pet.

Training Your Cat

Cats learn by watching. Therefore, teaching your cat tricks takes a lot of patience and repetition. Because cats normally scratch trees or the ground to remove the old nail casings on their claws, it is important the teach your cat to use a scratching post instead of your furniture.

Training Your Dog

Learning how to respond to basic obedience commands can literally save a dog's life in today's world of busy streets and fast automobiles. Obedience training can begin when dogs are 4 to 6 months old and continue throughout a dog's lifetime. Obedience-trained dogs make better pets, have fewer behavioral problems, and generally bond more closely with their owners.

There are many training methods, some more effective than others. A good trainer can help you figure out what works best with your dog. This can be an excellent way to train your pet and to improve your own skills. If you decide to do this, enroll your dog once it has been vaccinated. Ask your veterinarian for help in picking a class that matches your dog's abilities.

Whatever training program you pick, make sure you stick to it. In some cases, if you apply a little of this program and a little of that one, you can confuse your pet and diminish the effectiveness of the training. The most important part of training your dog is consistency and fairness.

Breeding Tropical Fish

Breeding tropical fish can be an interesting and fascinating project. Breeding egg-bearers is generally considered a project for the experienced aquarist. As a beginner, start with live-bearers.

A female live-bearer drops live fry, not eggs. She might eat those fry if you do not take certain precautions. To assist you in raising fry, use a breeding trap that fits on the inside of your aquarium. When a female is ready to give birth, put her in the trap. Return the female to the aquarium the day after the fry are born. Keep the young fish in the trap until they are too big for adult fish to swallow.

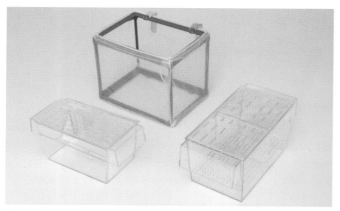

Because breeding traps greatly restrict movement, put the pregnant female in the trap only when she appears ready. Look for a plump belly, dark triangular mark (called a gravid spot) behind the anal fin, and an air bubble below the mark. Sometimes, you will be able to see the eyes of the unborn fry shortly before birth.

If you have an unused tank, fill it with aged water and use it as a maternity ward. Plant it with live or plastic plants, or attach a breeding trap to the tank. Put the ready-to-bear female in the maternity tank. When the fry are born, remove the female and allow the young to hide among the plants.

Most young live-bearers can be fed finely powdered, dry fish food. Small sifted daphnia, newly hatched brine shrimp, or microworms are good food for young fish. Increase the size of the food as your fish grow.

Fish Breeding Tips

1. Keep the young of similar species separated.
2. Plan ahead—make sure you have enough aquarium space for your new arrivals.

Breeding Goldfish

Breeding goldfish is not hard, but it is best to use fish that are 3 to 4 years old. A female that is ready to lay eggs will have an enlarged body, and the male will have little white pellets or bumps on his fins and gills. As he chases her, she will scatter 500 or more eggs. He will fertilize the eggs, which will sink and cling to plants or ornaments in your tank. The eggs are almost invisible, but you can see them if you look closely.

When the parents settle down, put the adults into a separate tank, or remove the plants and ornaments to which the eggs are attached and put them into a separate tank. If you do not separate the eggs from the adult fish, the eggs and the babies will be eaten. The eggs—not all of them—will hatch in three to six days. At 6 weeks old, the fry will look like real fish.

Feed the new arrivals a finely powered goldfish food, newly hatched brine shrimp, or sifted daphnia.

Breeding Budgies

To breed your budgie, you will need a breeding cage, a nest box to hang in the cage, and nesting food to supplement the female's diet. These are available at most pet shops.

A male budgie should be 10 months old or older before his first mating; a female should be at least 1 year old. The mate for your bird should come from a reliable source and should be healthy and active.

The female can lay as many as seven eggs, but not all on the same day. The eggs hatch 18 to 20 days after the first one is laid. Leave the parents alone during this period. Never disturb the nest.

Plan to breed your bird after March or April. Warm weather is best for the baby birds.

You had one budgie, now you have five. What are you going to do with them? For the birds' sake, make sure they get good homes.

Baby budgies start to grow feathers about two weeks after they are hatched. They will have all of their feathers in four to five weeks.

The parents will feed their young. But, once the young start pecking for themselves (about one week after hatching), put them in a separate cage from their parents. Do this first thing in the morning.

Training Your Budgie

A budgie will pick up plenty of tricks on its own. But if you hold regular sessions and offer rewards for successful learning, you will have a truly educated bird. Teach your budgie four things: how to perch, how to hold on with its beak, how to climb, and how to descend. Once your bird masters these, you can teach it all kinds of tricks.

Brainy Birds

To teach a trick, first show your budgie what to do. Develop a motion, such as snapping your fingers, for each trick you want the bird to learn. Your bird will soon associate that motion with the trick. Reward the bird's successes with a treat, such as a piece of soda cracker.

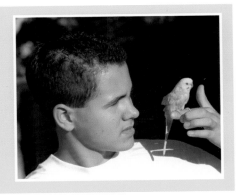

To teach your budgie how to hold things in its beak, simply hold the bird in your hand and gently push its beak over a small round stick. Make sure the stick is not too thick—1/8 inch in diameter is OK. Soon your budgie will be pushing and pulling all kinds of small toys.

Parakeets love to climb, so give your bird a ladder. Put the budgie on the first rung, and if it does not start climbing, give the bird a boost under the tail. It soon will go right up the ladder. When the bird gets to the top, reward it, and then turn it around. The bird will not go down as easily as it went up. But, do not forget to reward it when it does.

Teaching your bird to talk would be quite a trick, wouldn't it? You can do it, but it will take patience. The earlier you start, the better. The bird should be tame, and if possible, younger than 6 months old. Teaching an older bird to talk is possible but more difficult. Only one person should do the teaching.

Hold regular sessions in the quiet of your room. Do not surprise your budgie during the session. Sudden noise, movement, or changes in light will scare the bird. Start with one or two words. It may take two or three months for your pet to learn these. Talk loudly and slowly, and use the same pitch and pronunciation each time you speak. A high-pitched voice seems to get the best results. Make your sessions short, stopping when your budgie

If you are tempted to teach your bird to whistle, wait until you have taught it to talk. Once it learns how to whistle, it might not want to learn how to talk.

gets tired or bored. Budgies learn by repetition, so repeat the words and phrases over and over.

After you have taught your pet several words, come back to the first words it learned or it might forget them. Keep talking with your budgie once it learns to speak or it will forget all that it has learned.

Budgies do not talk as well as parrots or mynah birds. Do not be disappointed if your pet's speech is somewhat garbled. Although your budgie might never learn to say "Polly wants a cracker," with patience and persistence, you can teach the bird several words and simple phrases.

Breeding Canaries

About all you need for breeding canaries is a breeding cage, a little common sense, and a healthy mate for your bird.

Breed canaries only in the spring. In April or May, put some paper in the female's cage. If she proceeds to tear it up, and if she calls to the male bird, put them both in the breeding cage. Remove the divider once the male shows signs of courting.

If they fight, replace the divider for a day and try again. Give them some privacy. Drape a cloth over the nest end of the cage. You can use nesting material like 2-inch-thick string wool or cloth ravelings, but avoid any fine synthetic fibers or thread that might entangle feet, toes, or other body parts.

Canary Breeding Tips

1. Take out the male if he annoys the female.

2. Feed nesting birds egg food and conditioning seeds.

3. At night, once the lights are off near the cage, leave them off; do not disturb the birds at night.

4. Remove any broken eggs.

5. Check the nest daily to see if you need to add more nesting material.

A breeding cage has a divider that separates the male and female. When the male begins to sing and court the female, you can remove the divider.

Give baby canaries all the egg food (available at pet stores) and conditioning food they want. But, do not hand-feed them; the mother will do it. The babies will start eating without help in about five weeks. They will lose their first feathers (the fuzz) in two to four months. At that time you can start them on regular mixed canary seed. In a year's time, you will have a cage full of adult canaries that you might be able to sell.

Training Your Canary

A canary is easy to train. You can teach your bird to perch on a T-stick and then on your fingers. Once you and your canary become pals, open the cage door and hold the T-stick in the cage. In time, the bird will hop onto the stick. Once the canary learns to stay there, slowly draw the bird and the stick out of the cage. Make sure all the windows, shades or blinds, and doors are closed in case the bird flies off the stick. Also, be sure no ceiling fans are in use. Do not chase the bird if it flies. Simply leave the cage door open and the bird will return when it is ready.

A male canary will learn to sing on its own or from another canary when it matures. This is not a skill you have to teach your bird.

Breeding Guinea Pigs

It is not difficult to raise a family of guinea pigs. Newborn guinea pigs have all their fur, open eyes, and can eat solid food within the first day. However, they might nurse for two to three weeks.

The sow should be very young when she breeds. It is best to breed before she is 10 months old because at that age her pelvic bones fuse, which makes delivery more difficult.

When you think the sow is pregnant, put her in a separate pen. The time between breeding and birth (gestation time) is between 59 and 72 days. You can expect between one and six babies in a litter. Keep the sow and her youngsters in separate quarters because the sow might be ready to breed again shortly after the litter is born.

Once your bird is trained to perch on a T-stick, try substituting your finger. Always work and move slowly when training your bird.

Female guinea pigs are called sows; the males are called boars. When breeding guinea pigs, do not put two boars with a group of sows because the boars will fight too much.

Guinea pigs can be weaned once they are 3 weeks old. To wean them, simply take the young from the sow and put them in new pens. Separate the males from the females. Return the sow to her regular pen a week after weaning.

Keep in mind that guinea pigs can produce a large number of offspring that can themselves start reproducing in a short time. Nobody really wants to be overrun by guinea pigs.

Showing Guinea Pigs

Guinea pigs are exhibited at some county and state farm shows. You might also be able to enter your guinea pig in a local community show. Competition with other guinea pigs will teach you a lot more about raising and selecting a guinea pig. Deformities, missing toenails, unmatched eyes, improper hair color, plucked hair, and evidence of disease are some of the faults that might disqualify a guinea pig from the showring.

Breeding Hamsters

If you have room for about eight more hamsters, or have a bunch of friends who want hamsters, give breeding a try. However, be aware that once you start breeding hamsters they will produce many, many offspring very quickly. Make sure you have homes for them before you begin.

The following instructions will help you decide when to breed your pets. A female should be at least 8 weeks old to breed, and a male should be 2 to 3 months old. Put the prospective parents together in the evening. (Always put the female into the male's cage. If you bring a male to the female, she will consider him an intruder and start fighting. If they start to fight, separate them.) Try again the next evening. Once they stop fighting leave them together for about a week.

Baby hamsters will arrive in 15 to 18 days. They will be born hairless and helpless. Do not handle them even if they seem to be lost from their mother. She eventually will round them up. She might carry a baby in the pouch of her mouth, so do not get worried if you see her put one there. Do not disturb the mother or the litter for the first week. Litter abandonment and cannibalism are fairly common if the mother is disturbed too much. After the first week, remove the soiled bedding from the cage. In seven to 10 days, you can put out food for the babies. Put softened hamster pellets directly on the floor of the cage. Clean up the uneaten food daily. Make a small water tube (sipper) available to the babies at this time.

Leave the babies with their mother for about 26 days. When you take out the litter, separate the males and females. Give the mother four days of additional rest.

Breeding Mice

Mice can be bred after they are 4 months old. It takes only 20 days for a female to produce a litter, and that litter might contain 12 mice. If you choose to breed mice, make sure you will have homes for the new arrivals. A pet shop might take some.

The babies will be born blind and hair-less but will grow up in three to four weeks. Leave the babies alone to let the mother care for them. If you interfere, she might destroy the newborns. About all you need to do is provide a nest. This can be a small box about 4 inches square with a 2-inch opening. Hinge the top to make it easy to clean. Separate the mother from the male after the litter is born to prevent them from breeding again. Also, the male might destroy the baby mice if left in the same cage with them.

Guidelines for Responsible Pet Owners

- Observe all laws, ordinances, and neighborhood rules regarding pets.
- Spay or neuter all dogs and cats that will not be used for breeding.
- Give your pet the proper nutrition, exercise, housing, and veterinary care as required.
- Be courteous; respect the property of others.
- Always dispose of wastes and bedding in a proper manner, and always practice good personal sanitation.

Resources for Pets

Scouting Literature

Animal Science, Bird Study, Dog Care, Fish and Wildlife Management, Horsemanship, Mammal Study, Reptile and Amphibian Study, and *Veterinary Medicine* merit badge pamphlets

Visit the Boy Scouts of America's official retail Web site at *http:// www.scoutstuff.org* for a complete listing of all merit badge pamphlets and other helpful Scouting materials and supplies.

Books

Anderson, Jane, et al. *Pet's Best Friend: What Animals Say About Their Kids.* Tallfellow Press, 2001.

Chrystie, Frances N. *Pets.* 4th ed. Little, Brown, and Co., 1995.

Stein, Sara. *Great Pets: An Extraordinary Guide to Usual and Unusual Family Pets.* Workman Publishing, 1974.

BIRDS

Rach, Julie, and Gary A. Gallerstein. *First Aid for Birds: An Owner's Guide to a Happy Healthy Pet.* Hungry Minds, 1998.

Spadafori, Gina, and Brian L. Speer. *Birds for Dummies.* John Wiley and Sons, 2001.

Wolter, Annette, et al. *Parakeets: Everything About Purchase, Care, Nutrition, Breeding, and Behavior.* Barrons Educational Series, 1999.

CATS

Fogle, Bruce. *The New Encyclopedia of the Cat.* DK Publishing, 2001.

Smith, Carin A. *101 Training Tips for Your Cat.* Dell Publishing, 1994.

Spadafori, Gina, and Paul D. Pion. *Cats for Dummies.* Hungry Minds, 1997.

DOGS

Baer, Ted. *How to Teach Your Old Dog New Tricks.* Barrons Educational Series, 1991.

Kilcommons, Brian, and Sarah Wilson. *Good Owners Great Dogs.* Warner Books, 1999.

Rutherford, Clarice, and David H. Neil. *How to Raise a Puppy You Can Live With.* Alpine Publications, 1999.

FISH

Axelrod, Herbert, et al. *Dr. Axelrod's Mini-Atlas of Freshwater Aquarium Fishes.* TFH Publications, 1996.

Boruchowitz, David E. *The Simple Guide to Fresh Water Aquariums.* TFH Publications, 2001.

Fairfield, Terry. *A Commonsense Guide to Fish Health.* Barrons Educational Series, 2000.

Sandford, Gina. *An Essential Guide to Choosing Your Tropical Freshwater Fish.* Barrons Educational Series, 2000.

SMALL ANIMALS

Curran, Wanda L. *Your Guinea Pig: A Kid's Guide to Raising and Showing.* Storey Books, 1995.

Von Frisch, Otto. *Hamsters.* Barrons Educational Series, 1998.

Vanderlip, Sharon L. *Mice.* Barrons Educational Series, 2001.

OTHER PETS

Bartlett, Richard D., and Patricia P. Bartlett. *Lizard Care from A to Z.* Barrons Educational Series, 1997.

Kanable, Ann. *Raising Rabbits.* Rodale Press, 1981.

Palika, Liz. *The Complete Idiot's Guide to Reptiles and Amphibians.* Alpha Books, 1998.

Searle, Nancy, and Gwen Steege. *Your Rabbit: A Kid's Guide to Raising and Showing.* Storey Books, 1992.

Organizations and Other Resources

Aquarium Fish, Bird Talk, Cat Fancy, and Reptiles magazines
BowTie, Inc.
P.O. Box 6050
Mission Viejo, CA 92690
Telephone: 949-855-8822
Web site:
http://www.animalnetwork.com

American Cat Fanciers Association
P.O. Box 1949
Nixa, MO 65714-1949
Telephone: 417-725-1530
Web site: http://www.acfacat.com

American Humane
63 Inverness Drive East
Englewood, CO 80112
Telephone: 303-792-9900
Web site:
http://www.americanhumane.org

American Kennel Club
Telephone: 212-696-8200
Web site: http://www.akc.org

The American Society for the Prevention of Cruelty to Animals
424 East 92nd St.
New York, NY 10128-6804
Telephone: 212-876-7700
Web site: http://www.aspca.org

The Humane Society of the United States
2100 L St., NW
Washington, DC 20037
Telephone: 202-452-1100
Web site: http://www.hsus.org

SPAY/USA
25 Davis Ave.
Port Washington, NY 11050
Toll-free telephone: 800-248-7729
Web site: http://www.spayusa.org

Acknowledgments

The Boy Scouts of America gives special thanks to Boy Scout Advancement Committee member Steve Bowen, D.V.M., for his assistance with this new edition of the *Pets* merit badge pamphlet. We appreciate his time and expertise. Dr. Bowen is a practicing veterinarian in El Centro, California.

The BSA extends thanks to the following individuals, who contributed to the 1984 edition of this pamphlet, upon which this new edition is based: Dr. Alice M. Wolf, Department of Small Animal Medicine and Surgery, College of Veterinary Medicine, Texas A&M University; Dr. H. W. Weicht, Brown Trail Animal Clinic, Bedford, Texas; and Guy Hodge, director of Data and Information Services, the Humane Society of the United States.

Dr. Steve Bowen

Photo Credits

Beth Blair, courtesy—page 18

Budgies.org, courtesy—pages 33 and 56

Hamsterific.com, courtesy—page 45 *(top)*

©Photos.com—cover *(all except grooming items, hamster ball, mouse)*; pages 7, 9, 17, and 19

Shirley L. Sharp, http://freshaquarium. about.com, courtesy—pages 26 *(bottom)*, 27 *(top)*, 28 *(both)*, and 30 *(both)*

All other photos not mentioned above are the property of or are protected by the Boy Scouts of America.

Brian Payne—pages 4–6 *(all)*, 8, 10, 12–13 *(both)*, 20 *(both)*, 32, 34, 37–39 *(all)*, 42 *(top)*, 43 *(photo)*, 49–50 *(both)*, 55, 57 *(both)*, 59, and 64

Randy Piland—pages 22 and 24

Steve Seeger—pages 16 and 42 *(bottom)*